Hi, my name's Anna and I'm a student at college. I like my teacher, Mr Taylor, but sometimes he really gets on my nerves!

Most of the time he is very helpful. But some days he makes me feel stupid. Today I was trying to do some hard maths. "Come on," he said, "you can do this, I know you can."
But I couldn't and I felt awful.

Everyone else seemed to be able to do it.
"Come on," he said, "I'll show you again."
He showed me again but I still couldn't do it.
I felt really stupid.
Then what did he do? He went off to help someone else!
He just left me there!

"There's no need to feel stupid just because you don't understand something," said Mr Taylor.
"I don't understand *Doctor Who*. Everyone else seems to."

I waited for him to come back. He took ages helping other people. So I got up and went to the canteen.

"You don't understand *Doctor Who*? But that's easy!"

In the canteen I had a drink and calmed down a bit.
But then Mr Taylor came in and had a go at me for leaving the class!
He made me go back to the lesson.
I was really annoyed.
He treats me like I'm a kid.

When I got back John and Omar had finished their work.
Mr Taylor told them they'd done really well.
He never tells me I've done well.
They said thanks for helping them.
That's not fair! He helped them finish it.
He didn't help me finish it.

At last! He came back to help me and he showed me again.

This time I did it and got it right.

"Now I understand!" I said.